Investigations

Cooling

Patricia Whitehouse

www.raintreepublishers.co.uk
Visit our website to find out more information about **Raintree** books.

To order:
☎ Phone 44 (0) 1865 888112
▤ Send a fax to 44 (0) 1865 314091
▯ Visit the Raintree Bookshop at **www.raintreepublishers.co.uk** to browse our catalogue and order online.

First published in Great Britain by Raintree,
Halley Court, Jordan Hill, Oxford OX2 8EJ,
part of Harcourt Education.
Raintree is a registered trademark of Harcourt
Education Ltd.

Editorial: Diyan Leake and Richard Woodham
Design: Michelle Lisseter
Picture Research: Maria Joannou
Production: Jonathan Smith

Originated by Dot Gradations Ltd
Printed and bound in China by
South China Printing Company

ISBN 1 844 43671 3 (hardback)
08 07 06 05 04
10 9 8 7 6 5 4 3 2 1

ISBN 1 844 43676 4 (paperback)
09 08 07 06 05
10 9 8 7 6 5 4 3 2 1

British Library Cataloguing in Publication Data
Whitehouse, Patricia
Cooling. – (Investigations)
536.4
A full catalogue record for this book is available
from the British Library.

Acknowledgements
The publishers would like to thank the
following for permission to reproduce
photographs: Heinemann Library pp. **4–13**,
18–22 (Robert Lifson); PhotoEdit pp. **14–17**
(Michael Newman).

Cover photograph of children playing in water
reproduced with permission of Corbis (Ed Cook)

Every effort has been made to contact copyright
holders of any material reproduced in this book.
Any omissions will be rectified in subsequent
printings if notice is given to the publishers.

The paper used to print this book comes from
sustainable resources.

Contents

Some words are shown in bold, **like this.**
You can find them in the glossary on page 23.

What is cooling?

Cooling takes away heat.

Some places are good for cooling.

When something cools, it might feel different.

It might change shape.

Can cooling change wet things?

Pour some juice in an ice-cube tray.

The juice is a **liquid**.

Put the tray in the freezer.

Does cooling change juice?

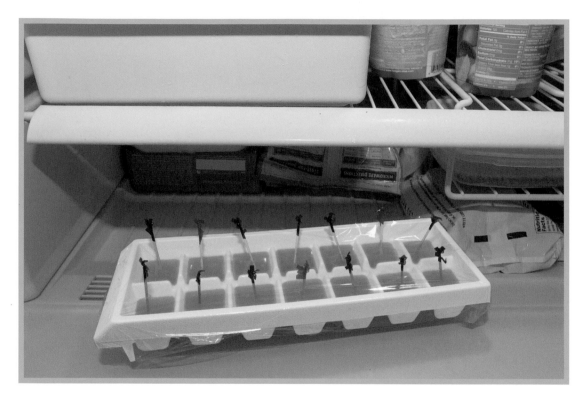

The freezer is a cold place.

The juice will get cold, too.

When the juice gets cold enough, it **freezes**.

It becomes a **solid**.

Can cooling change soft things?

These biscuits just came out of a hot oven.

They are hot and soft.

Put the biscuits on a plate.

What will happen to the biscuits now?

Does cooling change biscuits?

The plate is cooler than the oven.

The biscuits will cool, too.

Biscuits get hard as they cool.

Now they are ready to eat.

Can cooling change hard things?

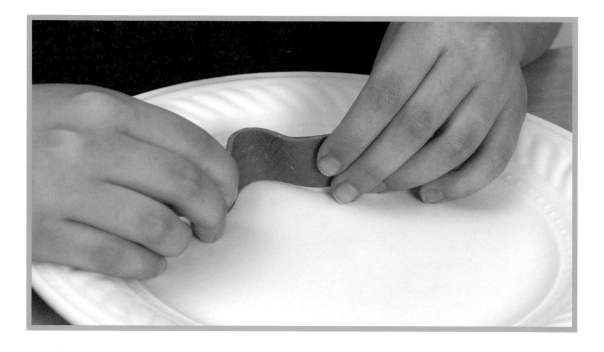

This stick of gum is **solid**.

It can bend, though.

Put the gum in the freezer for a few hours.

What happens to the gum?

Does cooling change gum?

The freezer is a cold place.

The gum will get cold, too.

Very cold gum is **brittle**.

It breaks apart easily.

Can cooling change air?

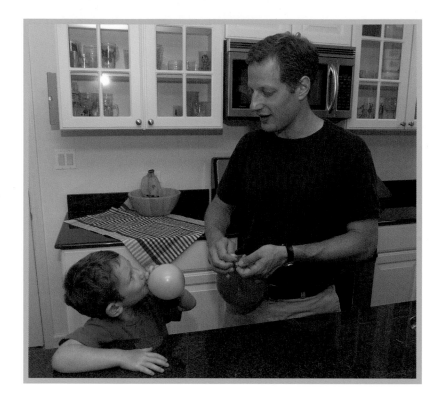

Blow up two balloons until they are the same size.

Tie a knot in the ends to keep the air in!

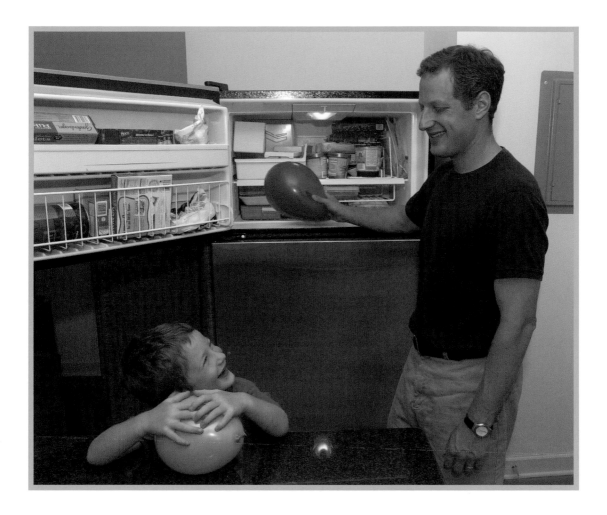

Put one balloon in the freezer for a few days.

Leave the other balloon on the counter.

Does cooling change the balloon?

The freezer is a cold place.

The air in the balloon gets cold.

The balloon gets smaller as it gets cold.

Did the balloon on the counter get smaller?

Quiz

Which has been cooled the most?

How can you tell?

Look for the answer on page 24.

Glossary

brittle
breaks easily

freeze
change from a liquid to a solid

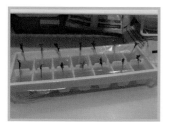

liquid
something wet that can be poured

solid
something hard that has a shape

Index

Answer to quiz on page 22

The ice cubes have been cooled the most. They are frozen solid.